HOME ON THE RANGE

John A. Lomax
and His
Cowboy Songs

by
Deborah Hopkinson

illustrated by
S. D. Schindler

❖ G. P. PUTNAM'S SONS ❖

For Bonnie and Jamie, my Texas family — D.H.

G. P. PUTNAM'S SONS

A division of Penguin Young Readers Group.

Published by The Penguin Group. Penguin Group (USA) Inc., 375 Hudson Street, New York, NY 10014, U.S.A. Penguin Group (Canada), 90 Eglinton Avenue East, Suite 700, Toronto, Ontario M4P 2Y3, Canada (a division of Pearson Penguin Canada Inc.). Penguin Books Ltd, 80 Strand, London WC2R 0RL, England. Penguin Ireland, 25 St. Stephen's Green, Dublin 2, Ireland (a division of Penguin Books Ltd.). Penguin Group (Australia), 250 Camberwell Road, Camberwell, Victoria 3124, Australia (a division of Pearson Australia Group Pty Ltd). Penguin Books India Pvt Ltd, 11 Community Centre, Panchsheel Park, New Delhi - 110 017, India. Penguin Group (NZ), 67 Apollo Drive, Rosedale, North Shore 0632, New Zealand (a division of Pearson New Zealand Ltd). Penguin Books (South Africa) (Pty) Ltd, 24 Sturdee Avenue, Rosebank, Johannesburg 2196, South Africa. Penguin Books Ltd, Registered Offices: 80 Strand, London WC2R 0RL, England.

Design by Richard Amari.

Text set in Edwardian Medium and Dyadis Bold Italic.

Library of Congress Cataloging-in-Publication Data

Hopkinson, Deborah. Home on the range : John A. Lomax and his cowboy songs / written by Deborah Hopkinson ; illustrated by S. D. Schindler. p. cm. 1. Lomax, John Avery, 1867–1948—Juvenile literature. 2. Ethnomusicologists—United States—Biography—Juvenile literature. 3. Folk songs, English—United States—History and criticism—Juvenile literature. I. Schindler, S. D. ill. II. Title. ML3930.L62H66 2009 782.421642092—dc22 [B] 2008016802

ISBN 978-0-399-23996-0

1 3 5 7 9 10 8 6 4 2

COWBOY GRACE

◆

Eat your meat and save the skin;
Turn up your plates and let's begin.

THE TEXAS COWBOY

❖

O, I am a Texas cowboy,
Far away from home;
If ever I get back to Texas
I never more will roam.

JOHN AVERY LOMAX grew up singing. Why, he probably knew more folk songs, tunes, and ballads than there were cattle in the great state of Texas.

Whenever his father hollered "Plantin' time," young John would run barefoot behind the plow, dropping bright kernels of corn onto the sweet dark earth.

"Keep up, now!" urged his father. And so John sang in time to his work:

Whistle and hoe,
Sing as you go;
Shorten the rows
By the songs you know.

John knew songs to make other chores easier, too. When his mother called "Time to churn the butter," John got out the old wooden churn and pulled the dasher up and down until his arms felt ready to fall off. But he got the job done, singing:

Come, butter, come; come, butter, quick,
For old Aunt Kate's a-waitin' at the gate,
For a piece of johnnycake.
Come, butter, come!

Before long, John was singing the sun awake in the morning and crooning the moon to sleep at night. And sometimes, with his good friend Nat Blythe, John sang just for fun:

Oh, rabbit skipped and rabbit hopped,
Oh, rabbit eat my turnip top,
Oh, rabbit, rabbity hash.

The Lomax family farm was nestled near a river on the old Chisholm Trail. In those days cowboys still drove cattle along the trail, and they often stopped to rest near John's house. Just as John sang in time to his chores, the cowboys made up songs to pass the long hours in the saddle and the cold, lonely nights.

Sometimes, when John lay in his small attic bed, he could hear the mournful voice of a cowboy in the distance.

Whoo-oo-oo-ee-oo-oo, whoo-oo whoo-whooo-oo
O, slow up, dogies, quit your roving around,
You have wandered and tramped all over the ground;
O graze along, dogies, and feed kinda slow,
And don't forever be on the go—
O move slow, dogies, move slow.

The songs went straight to John's heart, and he made up his mind to write down each and every cowboy song he heard.

John didn't have much to write with, so he used whatever came to hand—the stub of a pencil, scraps of paper, cardboard torn from a box. He kept his roll of songs safe in the bottom of a trunk, tied up with string.

I'm a poor, lonesome cowboy,
And a long ways from home.

SOMETIMES one of the hardest things in life is to find the right path. John wasn't sure where his road would lead, but he loved learning and books just as fiercely as he loved music. So when he grew up, John left home, and by working hard to earn money, he was able to enter the University of Texas.

One day, John got the courage to show his precious collection of cowboy songs to his teacher. He hoped the professor would find them as fascinating as he did.

But that snooty professor just turned up his nose. "There's nothing of value in these songs of plain, ordinary folk," he sneered.

John felt his face go red. He rushed away, ashamed and embarrassed. That night he made a fire and burned every last scrap of song.

I'm going to leave old Texas now,
For they've got no use for the longhorn cow;...

JOHN never forgot his professor's cruel words. But he went on to finish college and become a teacher. Several years later John got a chance to go back to school at Harvard University in Massachusetts. There he met a teacher who changed his life.

Professor Barrett Wendell was tired of teaching from the same old books, so he asked John and the other students to do something fun and new: to write a long paper about their own part of the country, about the place they called home. And, of course, to share it in class!

Home! To John, home would always be Texas, and home would always be about singing. Even if the other students laughed, John knew he had to write his paper about cowboy songs.

John wanted his project to be great. Even though he knew lots of songs, he figured there must be lots more he didn't know. So he wrote to newspapers all over the West, asking for help from readers.

John asked folks to send him old ballads they'd heard from grandparents. He asked for songs about the deeds of desperadoes, the stories of stage drivers, and, of course, cowboy songs.

Come all you jolly cowboys that follow the bronco steer,
I'll sing to you a verse or two your spirits for to cheer; . . .

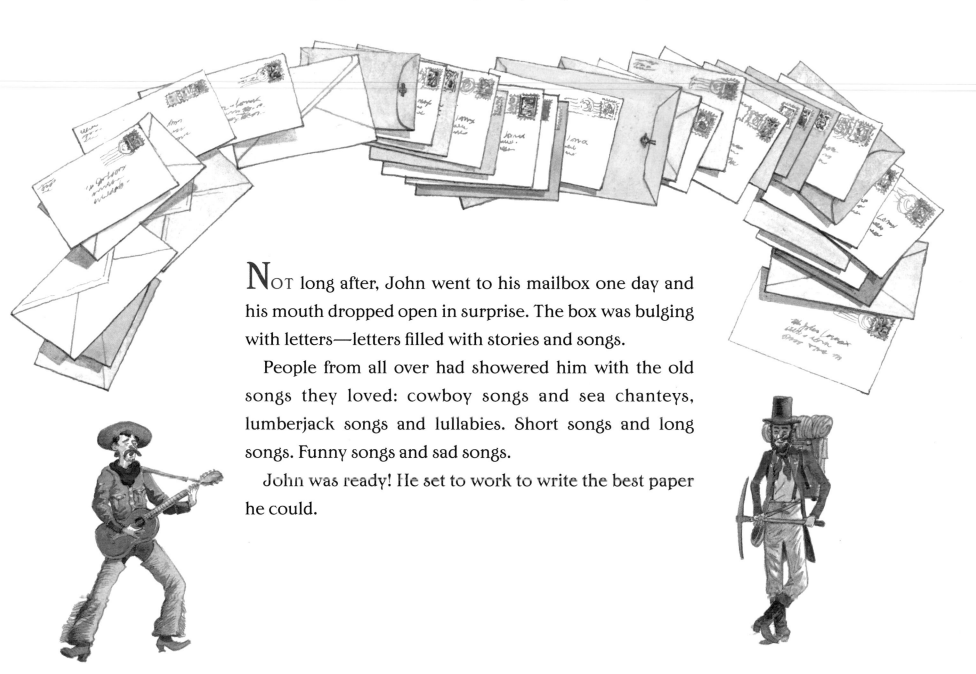

NOT long after, John went to his mailbox one day and his mouth dropped open in surprise. The box was bulging with letters—letters filled with stories and songs.

People from all over had showered him with the old songs they loved: cowboy songs and sea chanteys, lumberjack songs and lullabies. Short songs and long songs. Funny songs and sad songs.

John was ready! He set to work to write the best paper he could.

When it came John's turn to present his work to the class, he hoped his teacher and friends wouldn't laugh. John cleared his throat nervously. He told his classmates about his farm by the old Chisholm Trail, and how he'd grown up hearing cowboys sing to their cattle in the starry darkness of a deep Texas night.

John said he didn't know who wrote most of the songs he had collected. "They seem to have sprung up as quietly and mysteriously as grass on the plains."

The room grew still when John began to sing. And as his friends listened, they suddenly forgot where they were. Why, it was almost as if they became cowboys themselves, telling tales around a flickering camp-fire after one more weary day on the trail.

"Lay still, little dogies, lay still," John said, just like a cowboy putting his
cattle to sleep. Then he gave a cowboy's long night-herding yodel.

At first there was a startled silence. Then, to John's delight, the whole
class burst into cheers.

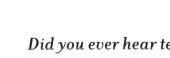

Did you ever hear tell of Sweet Betsy from Pike,
Who crossed the wide prairies with her lover Ike,
With two yokes of cattle and one spotted hog,
A tall Shanghai rooster and an old yaller dog?
Sing-too-ral-li-oo-ral-li-oo-ral-li-ay,
Sing-too-ral-li-oo-ral-li-oo-ral-li-ay.

AFTER that, John became determined to gather all the old cowboy songs he could find into a book. He wanted to record cowboys singing the songs, too, so he could give the recordings to a library to be kept for all time.

John set out with a notebook and a clumsy, heavy recording machine. It wouldn't be easy. No one else had ever collected American songs this way before. Like John's first professor, most people thought it was a crazy idea. And what would the cowboys think? John wasn't sure folks would be willing to sing into the Ediphone, his big, old-fashioned recording horn.

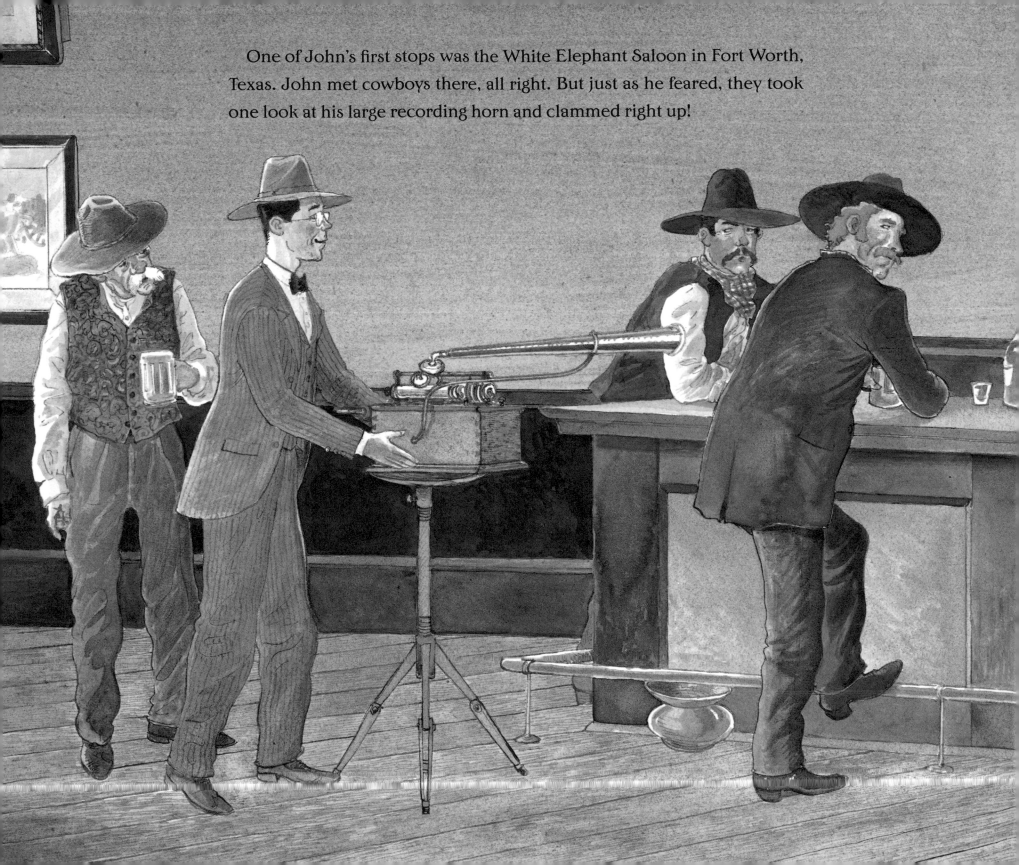

One of John's first stops was the White Elephant Saloon in Fort Worth, Texas. John met cowboys there, all right. But just as he feared, they took one look at his large recording horn and clammed right up!

"I've been singin' them songs ever since I was a kid. Everybody knows them," said one cattleman, shaking his head. "Only a fool would spend his time tryin' to set 'em down."

But John kept looking, and one night he met a cowboy who knew *eighty-nine* verses to "The Old Chisholm Trail." That's right: eighty-nine!

"That song is as long as the trail from Texas to Montana," the cowboy declared. But he went on, "I'm not goin' poke my face up to your blamed old horn and sing."

"Never mind the horn—at least sing it for me," pleaded John. And while
John scribbled the words, the cowboy crooned:

Come along, boys, and listen to my tale,
I'll tell you of my troubles on the old Chisholm Trail ...

I woke up one morning on the old Chisholm Trail,
Rope in my hand and a cow by the tail.

I'm up in the mornin' afore daylight
And afore I sleep the moon shines bright.

Not long after, John met a woman camping under some cotton-woods. She had wandered all over the West, telling fortunes and singing. Like the cowboys, she took one look at his recording machine and waved it away. Finally she let John write down the lyrics as her voice rang out sweet and clear:

Whoopee ti yi yo, git along, little dogies,
It's your misfortune and none of my own,
Whoopee ti yi yo, git along, little dogies,
For you know Wyoming will be your new home.

John was pleased with what he'd found. But he had only a few songs, and hardly any recordings. He needed more. Then he heard about an old trail cook in San Antonio who knew a world of cowboy songs. John headed there as soon as he could.

John found the cowboy asleep under a mesquite tree. The old cook lifted his hat, opened one eye, and closed it again. "Come back tomorrow," he mumbled crossly.

He'll never sing for me, thought John, discouraged. *Maybe I should just pack up and go home.*

But the next day John went back, determined to give it one more try. Suddenly, the old cook cleared his throat and crooned an unforgettable song into the recording horn:

Oh, give me a home where the buffalo roam,
Where the deer and the antelope play;
Where seldom is heard a discouraging word
And the skies are not cloudy all day.

Home, home on the range . . .

*How often at night when the heavens are bright
With the light of the glittering stars,
Have I stood here amazed and asked as I gazed
If their glory exceeds that of ours.*

BY the end of the summer, John had found enough songs for his book, and he'd gathered wonderful recordings, too.

One night before he went home, John sat with some cowboys around a bright, crackling fire. The men were quiet for a while, rolling the last of their coffee around in the bottom of their mugs. Then one by one, their voices drifted on the wind:

Feet in the stirrups and seat in the saddle,
And I hung and rattled with them longhorn cattle,
Coma-ti-yi-yipee, yippee yea, yippee yea,
Coma-ti-yi-yippee, yippee yea.

"Coma-ti-yippee, yippee yea," John sang along, his voice strong and happy. At the end he gave a cowboy yodel, and everyone laughed.

As John fell asleep under the starry sky, he smiled to think that someday, people not even born yet would be able to sing these songs, too. John had found his path in the world.

John Avery Lomax, song hunter, was on his way.

Music and songs are important parts of our lives. Through song we share stories about our families, our homes, our work, and our troubles.

While *Home on the Range* is historical fiction, it is based closely on the life of John Avery Lomax, an early pioneer in the collection of American folk music. This story traces how John got his start. But many of his best-known accomplishments took place much later in his life.

John was born in 1867. His first book, *Cowboy Songs and Frontier Ballads*, was published in 1910, when he was 43. This book helped preserve such favorite songs as "Git Along, Little Dogies," "Sweet Betsy from Pike," and most famously, "Home on the Range." Today "Home on the

Range" is the state song of Kansas and one of America's best-loved songs. But this song has a long and somewhat controversial history. When John first recorded it in 1910, he thought at first it was a folk song of unknown origins. After the song became popular in the 1930s, an Arizona couple claimed to have written it in 1905. Eventually, the song was traced to two Kansas men, Brewster Higley and Daniel E. Kelley, who wrote it in 1873. Finding the origins of songs can be difficult!

After his first book was published, John spoke and wrote about cowboy songs occasionally, but he also worked at other jobs to support his wife, Bess, and four children, John Jr., Shirley, Alan, and Bess. In May 1931, John's wife died. It was the Great Depression and times were hard. By the end of 1931, John, age 64, was out of work.

In early 1932, John and his eldest son, Johnny, came up with a daring plan. Johnny would drive his father around the country to earn money by giving lectures on cowboy songs. Once again, John became a song hunter. The next year he and his son Alan set off to collect songs for a new book. In the years to follow, John and Alan Lomax (and sometimes John's second wife, Ruby Terrill Lomax) drove thousands of miles through the countryside to record people singing the old songs they had learned from their parents and grandparents.

John was a pioneer who learned as he went along. Today people go to college to study proper methods of collecting songs, oral history, and folklore. But thanks to the Lomaxes, many wonderful songs were recorded and preserved for future generations. The Lomaxes were also instrumental in creating a national collection of folk music. Thousands of their recordings are part of the Archive of Folk Culture in the American Folklife Center at the Library of Congress. (John served as honorary consultant and curator of the archive beginning in 1933.) Among the well-known musicians the Lomaxes recorded and worked with were Jelly Roll Morton, Woody Guthrie, and Huddie Ledbetter, better known as Leadbelly. John A. Lomax published several collections of songs, as well as an autobiography, before his death in 1948 at the age of 80. Alan Lomax went on to become America's premier folk musicologist. Alan Lomax, who died in 2002, was named a National Treasure for his contributions to American folk music.

To learn more about folk music and the Lomaxes, you can visit the Library of Congress in person or the library's American Memory website. And don't forget to ask your parents, grandparents, and neighbors to teach you *their* favorite songs.

A NOTE ON SOURCES

❖

THIS story about John A. Lomax is based primarily on his autobiography, *Adventures of a Ballad Hunter* (New York: The Macmillan Company, 1947). Autobiographies are not always accurate, of course. So although I've included John's account of burning his cowboy song collection, readers may be interested to know that this incident is discounted (though not disproved) in Nolan Porterfield's biography, *Last Cavalier: The Life and Times of John A. Lomax, 1867-1948* (Urbana: University of Illinois Press, 1996). Lomax was a fascinating, complicated man.

Those interested in learning more about his later work may find *The Life and Legend of Leadbelly* by Charles Wolfe and Kip Lornell (New York: HarperCollins, 1992) especially helpful for insight into the complex relationship between Lomax and Leadbelly.

For an account of the origins of "Home on the Range," I referred to Kirke Mechem's article of the same title, which first appeared in the *Kansas Historical Quarterly* in November 1949 and has been reprinted in pamphlet form by the Kansas State Historical Society in Topeka.

OTHER WORKS CONSULTED

❖

Lomax, John A., and Alan Lomax. *Cowboy Songs and Other Frontier Ballads.* Revised and Enlarged. New York: The Macmillan Company, 1938.

Lomax, John A. *Songs of the Cattle Trail and Cow Camp.* New York: Duell, Sloan and Pearce, 1950. Illustrated edition prepared by Alan Lomax and Robin Roberts.

Lomax, John A., and Alan Lomax. *Our Singing Country: A Second Volume of American Ballads and Folk Songs.* New York: The Macmillan Company, 1941. Ruth Crawford Seeger, music editor.

Lomax, John A., and Alan Lomax. *Folk Song U.S.A.* New York: Duell, Sloan and Pearce, 1947. Charles Seeger and Ruth Crawford Seeger, music editors.